The Workbook and Planner
for the Serious Actor

by Leslie Becker

The Organized Actor®

the workbook and planner for the serious actor

© 2006 Leslie Becker
Triple Threat Ventures
Fifth Edition

Previously published in
© 2003 Fourth Edition
© 1999 Third Edition
© 1996 Revised Edition
© 1994 First Edition

This is a

Published by
Triple Threat Ventures, LLC
PO Box 231507
New York City 10023
Toll Free 866-347-0752
www.OrganizedActor.com

ISBN: 978-0-9667365-3-3

Printed in the United States by
Morris Publishing • 3212 East Highway 30 • Kearney, NE 68847

Here's what people are saying...

"THE ORGANIZED ACTOR® is an absolute must for any artist wishing to build and maintain a successful career. Leslie Becker uses her experience and provides actors with sensible planning tools and an overall agenda to keep organized and goal oriented." **Geoff Soffer,** Casting Manager, Major Television Network.

"Having worked both as a professional actress on Broadway and in education as Artistic Director of an arts conservatory, I know first-hand that THE ORGANIZED ACTOR® is an essential element in helping an artist make headway in this business. So often in our arts training we fail to also concentrate on the crucial industry dealings that are necessary for building relationships, assembling our materials, and presenting ourselves in the best light!" **Susan Egan**-Tony nominated actress and Director of Arts Conservatory

"To be successful in this business takes talent and organization. If you supply the talent...this book will supply the organization," **Kevin Stites,** Broadway Musical Supervisor, Fiddler on the Roof, Nine, Titanic and more

"The key to the business of show business is organization. Leslie Becker puts the responsibility for success where it belongs, squarely on the actor's shoulders." **Richard Sabellico,** Director and Acting Coach

"THE ORGANIZED ACTOR® is a fantastic tool for both the beginning and experienced actor. No serious professional should be without this comprehensive and motivational resource. The manual is a great way to ignite and direct one's career as an actor! And best of all - it is authored by an accomplished and savvy industry pro." **Marc Goldman,** New York University

"THE ORGANIZED ACTOR® delineates a very proactive approach to beginning a professional career--a concise and direct system for tracking, organizing and articulating the actor's goals and progress. I continually get feedback from our students who are still using it two and three years after graduation." **Henry Fonte,** Professor of Theatre, The Hartt School University of Hartford

"Thanks for publishing your wonderful book. The exercises are invaluable! I feel as if I have cleared away a years worth of debris-a true housecleaning of the creative process of acting!" **Vivian,** Los Angeles Actress, SAG, AFTRA, AEA

"What a great book! I threw away my old daytimer/calendar and only use THE ORGANIZED ACTOR® to keep track of everything for my career. I recommend this to anyone who is pursuing an acting career no matter what stage they are in." **Sherry,** NYC Actress, SAG, AEA

"This book is everything an actor will ever need, I was finding myself unorganized and not quite sure what I should be doing. I found THE ORGANIZED ACTOR® and things have made a complete turn around. Not only am I very set on what my goals are, I am more organized than I have every been in my whole life. This book isn't your everyday organizer. It's made with the actor in mind. Leslie Becker did a great thing for all actors when she wrote THE ORGANIZED ACTOR®. And her live seminars are like gold!" **Erik,** Bi-Coastal Actor, SAG, AFTRA, AEA

From the Author...

Dear Fellow Actor:

Thank you for purchasing **The Organized Actor**®. You are now part of a proactive group of artists who are choosing to run their acting careers like a business, and who are collectively changing the stereotype of a "starving actor." Back in 1994 I never would have guessed that **The Organized Actor**® would someday have a Fifth Edition. Back then, the idea for the book was merely a way to help my fellow actors. Now, more than a decade later, it continues to remain the #1 selling organizational tool for actors and growing everyday. This new 5th Edition is my favorite so far with a better calendar section that is sure to make you more productive, an expanded audition log with plenty of space to write, plus reworkings of all the sections you've become accustomed to including marketing, submissions, goal setting and more!

Since our last printing, our industry has seen major changes. My new 5th Edition reflects the growing necessity to be a smart and savvy business person in this competitive industry. And now, we've even got customized tabs you can order to give you easy access to all the sections in the book!

As I continue being a part of this magical industry, it never ceases to amaze me, frustrate me, delight me and challenge me. The strength I've found from remaining true to my own beliefs and values has helped me excel in many sides of the business...as a publicist and marketing director for various entertainment companies...as a director and choreographer...as producer of new musical theatre...and most importantly as an actor. My working knowledge of all aspects of the entertainment industry has strengthened my work as an actress and has taught me valuable lessons that have allowed me to flourish in the industry and in life. It thrills me that an idea created simply to give back has turned into an abundant source of inspiration for so many. You, the readers, have kept **The Organized Actor**® alive and built it stronger by asking for live seminars, additional books and one-on-one coaching!

So please accept my gracious thanks for keeping us alive for over a decade. May **The Organized Actor**® always be a mainstay in your arsenal of tools for your acting career. Carry this book wherever you go. Refer to it daily. Keep records. Take special notes in it. And most of all, think of it as your support system. For behind it lies a fellow actor who cares about you and wishes you continued success in this industry.

Again thank you. May you always continue your quest for stardom in all areas of your life.

Leslie Becker

Inside The Book...

Section 1: Goals and Strategic Plans
Goal Setting Workshop
Strategic Planning
Other Career Goals
Believing is Creating
What Do You Believe?

Section 2: Marketing
Positioning Yourself For Success
Fearless Actor Casting Quiz
Sample Cover Letters
Sample Postcards
Advice on Postcard Mailings
Sample Press Release
Correspondence Log

Section 3: Audition Log
Complete Audition Log

Section 4: Finances
Projected Budget
Income
Expenses by Category
Totals for Tax Season

Section 5: Industry Contacts
Phone Book by Category

Section 6: Calendar
Yearly Planner
52-week Calendar
Weekly Tallies
Inspirations on Each Page

This book belongs to...

your name	your numbers
emergency contact	
agent--legit	
agent--commercial	
agent--print	
agent	
agent	
manager	
attorney	
acting coach	
acting coach	
vocal coach	
doctor	
chiropractor	
dentist	
therapist	
hairstylist	
colorist	
other	
other	
other	

Goals and Strategic Plans

Making Your Dreams a Reality

Actors are wonderfully creative, versatile, passionate people! We abound with energy and spontaneity. But very often, the qualities that make us great in our work, make it difficult for us to focus and figure out who we really are and what we really want. I've met and worked with the full spectrum of actors from newbies to old pros. Across the board, the actors who are the most successful are the ones who are not afraid to say "This is who I am. This is what I want. And this is how I'm going to get it!"

You need a plan of action, some strong beliefs and the chutzbah to take action! And most importantly you need to realize that you're not only an artist, but also the CEO (Chief Executive Officer) of your business. As the CEO, you've got to take charge, make a plan and believe in your product...in this case it's you! You also need to know the market, know the competition and know what makes your product (you) special.

Because of the challenging facets of the industry that are undeniable, it is crucial that you BECOME A STRONG INDIVIDUAL SO THE HIGHS AND LOWS OF THE INDUSTRY ARE BALANCED BY A POSITIVE BELIEF IN YOURSELF. I believe that if you are determined to be successful you can be...as long as you make a plan and take consistent steps in the direction of your goals.

Notes...

Goal Setting Workshop

Knowing what you want out of your career is crucial. Until you know where you're going, it's impossible to figure out how you're going to get there. This Goal Setting Workshop will help you set attainable goals, devise a strategic plan on how to achieve them and set daily commitments that create the small steps for achieving your ultimate dreams.

I truly believe that human beings can achieve anything once they know what it is. It just takes three easy steps:
1) Decide what you want
2) Believe it's possible
3) Do it!

I know, I know, you're thinking "But I don't know what I want." I don't buy that. I believe you know exactly what you want down to the Nth detail but you're too afraid to say it because
a) you don't believe you can really get it
b) you see yourself *here* and want to be *there* but you have no idea how to get *there*, or
c) you are certain you can get anything you want. But if you do get everything you want, then what?

The bottom line is, you do know what you want. And now it's time to say it once and for all.

Do yourself a favor. Turn off the television. Unplug the telephone and give yourself one hour to go through the following process. I promise you, by going through these steps you will find a new sense of what you want and how you're going to achieve it! You owe it to yourself to dream in vivid color and create a compelling future. As you go through the process, you must open yourself to all possibility and not monitor yourself or question if something is possible or not. All things are possible during a goal setting workshop. Have fun! Just do it!

Answer this question...

If you woke up tomorrow and everything in your life was exactly as you would like it to be, what would it look like?

The Big Dream

Write down everything you see when your life is exactly as you want it. Where are you in your career? Who are the people you associate with on a daily basis? Who do you wake up next to? What does your house look like? What's the first thing you do when you awake? What are the feelings you experience on a daily basis? Don't question whether it's possible, just write down what you see!

Career Goals

So, you've decided what you want! Now you have to formulate a plan. Based on your big dream, create a list of goals that will get you closer to it. Those steps might include things like getting new headshots, studying with a certain teacher, playing a certain role, etc. Use this page only for career goals.

Financial Goals

Write down all things financial like paying down credit card debt, saving a certain amount each week, opening an individual retirement account, etc.

Personal Goals

Finally, write down personal goals. I believe we must create a balanced life. Learning to do things for our personal well being is crucial to our success in this business. Choose goals pertaining to your health, image, relationships, family, hobbies, contribution, etc.

My Top Goals

Now that you've written down many goals and aspirations, it's time to narrow down the ones that are most important to you right now...the dreams you are most passionate about and are willing to do whatever it takes to get there. Select three from your career goal list, one from your financial list and one from your personal list.

One of my career goals is:

Another of my career goals is:

My third career goal is:

My financial goal is:

My personal goal is:

Strategic Plan

So, you've figured out which goals are most important to you, now it's time to devise a plan of action.

1. Select one of your career goals and write it in the space below:

2. Now it's time to think logically. For example, if your long term goal is to star on Broadway in a Tony-Award winning musical, your strategic plan may include any of the following: study voice, dance and acting, star in local musical productions, move to New York, etc. If you're having trouble knowing where to start, think backwards. Begin as if you've already achieved the goal and work backwards.

3. Now write down three daily actions you are committed to doing EVERY SINGLE DAY that will help you take action on your strategic plan. For example, if your strategic plan includes studying voice, perhaps a daily action could be to vocalize EVERY DAY. Then go to the calendar section and schedule in when you'll do them and put them on your to do list.

1.

2.

3.

Strategic Plans

Do this process for each of your five goals on the following pages. Remember to work backwards as if you've already achieved your goal. That will help get you on your way. Don't edit yourself as you go. Think of the logical pattern to get there.

1. Select another of your career goals.

2. Devise a strategic plan.

3. Write down three daily actions you are committed to doing.

1.

2.

3.

1. Write down your third career goal.

2. Devise a strategic plan.

3. Write down three daily actions you are committed to doing.

1.

2.

3

1. Write down your financial goal.

2. Devise a strategic plan.

3. Write down three daily actions you are committed to doing.

1.

2.

3

1. Write down your personal goal.

2. Devise a strategic plan.

3. Write down three daily actions you are committed to doing.

1.

2.

3

Now that you've written these things down, help yourself stay committed to them by going to the calendar section right now and putting this week's commitments on your to-do list AND actually schedule them in on your calendar. You'll be amazed at how quickly you make progress. Congratulations! You are on the road to great success!

Other Career Goals

Once you've achieved the goals listed on the previous pages you'll certainly want to make new ones. Use these pages to list your new goals and plans. Once you've made goal achievement a priority in your life, you'll be amazed at how quickly things will happen. Good luck!

GOAL:

ACTION:

GOAL:

ACTION:

GOAL:

ACTION:

GOAL:

ACTION:

GOAL:

ACTION:

GOAL:

ACTION:

GOAL:

ACTION:

GOAL:

ACTION:

GOAL:

ACTION:

GOAL:

ACTION:

GOAL:

ACTION:

Believing is Creating

Deciding what you want and writing it down is only the first step to achieving success. But actually believing it is possible is crucial. If you don't truly believe you can achieve the things you want, then you're thwarting yourself at every step. Therefore you must create a set of beliefs that complement these terrific goals you have set for yourself. Beliefs create our reality. They have the power to inspire or inhibit; to help or hinder; to create success or failure.

You must be exceedingly careful about the thoughts you allow to circulate in your head. Everything you say and do on a consistent basis manifests into reality. So if you constantly say to yourself "You suck" your brain believes it for truth (whether it's true or not). So the next time you have a bad audition and ask yourself "Why did that happen?" Your brain proudly tells you, "Because you suck!" One of the most frequent things I hear actors say is "I don't audition well." Imagine if you said that everyday for a week. I'll guarantee by the end of the week you won't be auditioning well because you've convinced yourself that it's true.

The great thing about your brain is that only you have the power to program it. So why not program it with things that help you instead of hinder you. This isn't about arrogance, it's about necessity. Your brain is your most important tool to lead you to success. Beautifully programmed gray matter, combined with consistent action in the direction of your goals will always lead you on the right path.

GLOBAL BELIEFS: These are beliefs that begin with words like "I am," "People are," "The industry is." For example: "I am talented;" "The industry is a closed door to newcomers; " "I don't audition well."

RULE BELIEFS: These tend to be written in the form of a rule using the words "If...then." Examples: "If I only had the credits, then I could get a good agent." "If I was taller, then I would get more roles." "If I do what I love, then the money will come."

Take a minute to think about some things you hear yourself saying consistently. Be honest with yourself and you may discover that you have some inhibiting beliefs that are working against what you're trying to achieve.

What Do You Believe?

Write down some of the things you consistently say...both positive and negative about yourself and the industry.

I'm sure you found some negative beliefs that could be limiting you. What I'd like you to do now is take all of the negative beliefs you wrote down and turn them into positive ones. For example, if you did say "I don't audition well," change your belief to something like "I love to audition, because I love to perform." Be zany, outlandish. While you're at it, come up with some more positive beliefs as well. Create new beliefs that make you excited about things you weren't excited about before.

Hopefully these new ideas sound exciting to you and inspire you. Now pick your three most empowering ones to use consistently and write them down here.

1.

2.

3.

It's very possible that you're looking at these beliefs and feeling like all you did was write them down. How could that really make a difference? Well, you'll be shocked at what a difference these new beliefs can make. However, you will need to put in some work yourself. First, I challenge you to make several copies of your beliefs and put them in places where you will see them consistently. Secondly, begin to catch yourself in the old act. When you catch yourself saying something like "I don't audition well," correct yourself immediately by saying your new improved belief three or four times. I also challenge you to make your beliefs part of your morning and evening rituals. Say them out loud while you're in the shower, or getting dressed. Say them with conviction. It may sound silly, but putting your body into it and really believing what you're saying works. At the very least it gets you thinking in a positive way when you start the day! With daily practice your new beliefs will begin to take shape and you will be astounded at the results. If you're having difficulty coming up with some of your own, here are some of my favorites.

My talents are a privilege and a gift and I consistently use them in a positive way.
If I commit 100% to something, I shall reap the rewards.
I love to audition because it's an invitation to perform.
People are my greatest resource and I attract those who can help me in my career.
I am a star...I'm just enjoying my last moments of anonymity.
Everything that happens to me serves me for the positive in the future.

What's Great Now?

As we think about the things we don't have or where we would like to be, we often forget about the wonderful things we already possess. Learning to appreciate all the incredible wealth <u>you</u> already have in your life is crucial to reaching for more. So take a moment to write down all the things you are grateful for in your life.

Finally, think of three people in your life you are most grateful for and call them on the phone just to tell them how much they mean to you. I guarantee it will make the person receiving the call very happy and you will feel great all day long! Taking the time to do these things helps you remember what is really important in your life. Enjoy your day.

1.

2.

3.

The Mission

This is your one-stop reference page to keep you on track. I recommend photocopying this page and putting it in places where you will see it many times a day.

My top three dreams

1.

2.

3.

My three daily actions I am committed to EVERY DAY

1.

2.

3.

My top three current goals

1.

2.

3.

My top three empowering beliefs

1.

2.

3.

The three things I am most grateful for

1.

2.

3.

Marketing

Understanding Your Marketing and Promotion

A lot of actors think of themselves as creative people, not business people. But, as you've learned, being an actor is like running your own business...with you as the product. And what can make or break a business? Marketing! Regardless of whether or not you have an excellent agent and/or manager, it is still YOUR CAREER. And it is up to you to market yourself.

The following pages will not only help you create a marketing plan. They will also provide a place to keep track of who you send your materials to and view some sample cover letters, press releases and more. Keeping your face out there is crucial. I got a job once simply because my postcard was on their desk when they needed someone. Do not underestimate the power and importance of consistent and well thought-out marketing.

Two very important marketing tips:

PERSONALIZE: When sending photos and resumes, reels, letters, etc., always get a name with correct spelling of the person you're sending to. Never put "To Whom it may concern" or "Dear Agent." Be sure you call first to see if the agent still works at that agency. Agents jump around, so do your research.

THANK YOUS: After a particularly positive callback or interview, send a thank you note. This is simply common courtesy. I'm shocked to find out how few actors really do this. If you are new in the industry and trying to get your name and face out there, send one for each audition you have for a new casting person or theatre.

Notes...

Positioning Yourself

Acting is a business. You are selling a product and that product is YOU! There is no one else exactly like you on the face of the earth. But in this industry, you will be auditioning with people who fall into the same "type" as you. But, even if you look like someone else, YOU are still special. So, it's important that you market yourself in a unique and exciting way.

To do that, you can use a technique called positioning. The advertising industry uses it every day. It's the difference between the advertising campaigns for Mercedes and Volkswagon Beetle; Gap and Old Navy; McDonalds and Burger King. Each campaign selects a particular position of the market that they are seeking. It is quite easy to determine the positioning of each of these products. But, when the product is YOU, it is challenging because often we see ourselves differently than others do. POSITIONING YOURSELF THE WRONG WAY CAN KEEP YOU FROM A SUCCESSFUL ACTING CAREER. But, positioning yourself the right way gives you a unique identity and can lead you to the success you dream of.

To find out how the industry views you…ask. But wait! This quiz is not for the weak ego. This is for the actor who really wants authentic, helpful feedback. Don't take anything these people say personally. This is simply for gathering information. Use the following questions to ask your agent, a director or casting director you are close to, and two or three others whose opinion you respect. And of course, take the quiz yourself. Then compare notes. But be very selective about who you ask to take this test. Some people may feel put on the spot and may say no. An easy way to do this quiz is to send it via email to the folks who you know very, very well and who will be honest with you and ask if they would be willing to answer the questions for you. That makes it easy for them to say no and gives them time to do it without having to answer on the spot.

The Fearless Actor Casting Quiz

1. Name five roles you would get cast in right now? (Notice I said, "Get cast in" NOT "what you think you can play.")
2. What age range do you play?(Not how old you really are)
3. Three special qualities you bring to your roles.
4. Do you have any physical limitations that narrow your cast-ability?
5. What's one thing you really need to work on?
6. Does your "look" and photos/resumes really represent you?

Casting Quiz Responses

Since your opinion is the base point...what were your answers?

1. Five roles?

2. Age Range?

3. Three qualities you bring.

4. Physical limitations?

5. One skill to work on.

6. Does your look match the real you?

Once you have other people answer the questions. Then tabulate the results. What did you discover? Did you find that people see you the same way you see yourself? Or did you find that they thought you were much different? If they thought you were different, what did they think? And was it collective or just one or two that had the same opinion? If others see you as a great bad guy, but you think you're a young leading man, maybe you need to re-evaluate yourself. You may not like playing a bad guy, but you might be more successful doing it. It's that simple. Maybe all you need is a new physical image...a change of hair style or color, a weight loss or gain, or a new, distinctive wardrobe. A slight change can sometimes make all the difference!

Sample Cover Letter

SAMPLE A (Cover letter to agent)

Michael Nelson   *Always have the name of the agent with correct name spelling.*
Talent Associates
300 Sunset Blvd Suite 710
Los Angeles, CA 90069

Dear Michael: *If someone in the industry suggested you send this, point it out first and put it on the envelope too!*

Hello! Michelle Smith at ABC Casting suggested I send you my materials. She recently cast me in a national commercial and thought we'd make a great team.

Recently I...   *Bullet point a few key items to get their attention.*
• Starred as Joe Hardy in Damn Yankees at Paper Mill Playhouse.
• Had a featured role on Law and Order: SVU
• Filmed a national Pepsi commercical   *State specifically what you want and let them know you'll contact them.*

I'd like to set up an interview to meet in person. I'll call you next week to see when that would be possible in your schedule. I can be reached at (213) 888-0000 or use my self-addressed, stamped return postcard enclosed.   *Sample on following page.*

Thank you for your time! I look forward to hearing from you soon.

Sincerely,   *Thank them for their time and interest.*

John Doe   *Write a great P.S. about yourself. Sometimes that's all they read. Make it a winner!*

P.S. Be sure to watch me on Law and Order on Friday October 13 at 8 p.m. I'm Mr. McFarland's attorney.

SAMPLE B (Submission note) *Short. To the point. Thank them, tell them what you want and where they can reach you.*

Dear Michael:

Thank you for considering me for the role of Jack in INTO THE WOODS. I recently played the role at Cincinnati Playhouse and would love to bring him to life at your theatre. I can be reached at (213) 888-0000.

Thanks.

Jon Doe

P.S. Be sure to check out my website at www.JohnDoeActor.com

Sample Postcards

SAMPLE A: Return Postcard

Make it easy for them to mark a response.

Keep all of your comments in the positive so even if you get a "no," you don't feel rejected.

o   Yes, I've received your materials. Please call me right away to set up an interview_____

o   Yes, I've received your materials. If you don't hear from me in a week, give me a call._____

o   Yes, I've received your materials. You may not hear from us for a while. But if we are interested we will call you.

o   Yes, I've received your materials, and while I found them intriguing, I am not interested at this time.

Name_____

Agency_____

THANK YOU!

SAMPLE B: Announcement

Your Photo

JOE SLATER

Don't miss

Joe Slater
guest starring on

Law and Order

January 6, 2003
9 p.m. on CBS

Staying in Touch With the Industry

With technology bursting out of the seams, there is no excuse for not staying in touch with the industry. Facebook, Twitter, Linked In, YouTube and various other web-based programs allow you to keep your name and face out there easily and cost-effectively. However, you can't forget about the trusted snail mail as a more personalized way to reach out the industry. In fact, sending a photo and resume in the mail these days may actually be MORE effective than it was five years ago because so many people are simply opting for electronic submissions.

Regardless of the system you use, you must keep in touch with the industry on a consistent basis (every 4-6 weeks if you're a busy actor). You can do this through our fantastic mailing service that lets you create your own cards and postcards on-line, then automatically sends them to your recipients in the REAL MAIL. That means no more licking and stamping for you! Try out our system for free at www.LesliesCards.com. There are several packages available, or simply pay as you go. The system will let you store all of your contacts and you'll have a record of every card you ever send.

As for tips for your mailing updates:

1. Always honor requests. If someone asks you NOT to send them postcards, don't. If they say to send them, DO!

2. Always make your first mailing a headshot and resume with a very brief cover note.

3. Don't send a "global" postcard to the whole office. Personalize them for the specific person you auditioned for or have a relationship with. If you know several people in one office, send one to each of them.

4. Send your mailings (postcards or cards) every four to six weeks or when you have three pertinent bullet points to say.

Sample Press Release

As the publicist of your business you have to generate your own publicity. This can be done very inexpensively with the use of press releases and public service announcements. If you are in a show or making a guest appearance on a sitcom, or even directing a show for the local high school, you must publicize. The more your name gets out there, the quicker your fame will escalate. Below is a sample press release. Format: One side only, double spaced.

Attention grabbing banner that tells them it's important to read this now

FOR IMMEDIATE RELEASE

A headline that tells them what the release is about. ☞ Resident actress to star in "Proof"

For a local paper, the fact that you are a resident may be all it takes. ☞

First sentence must tell what article is about so they can decide right away if they should read further.

Long Island resident, Lyn Walker, will star as Catherine in PROOF May 6-22 at the Paper Mill Playhouse.

Walker, an active Long Island resident, has been acting professionally for nearly 20 years. She has won many awards for her performances including a Tony award for her portrayal of Rose in STREET SCENE and the Drama Desk for her "hysterically funny" portrayal of Amanda in PRIVATE LIVES. Other credits include Marian in THE MUSIC MAN, AIDA, Laura in THE GLASS MENAGERIE and BENT.

Tell them about other involvement with the community. ☞ Walker's directing talents have been seen at Bellport High in GUYS AND DOLLS, TO KILL A MOCKINGBIRD, 42ND STREET and STREET SCENE and she's a member of Bellport Help.

Don't miss Bellport's own star, Lyn Walker, in PROOF May 6-22 at the Papermill Playhouse 320 S. Bend Drive in New Jersey.

For tickets call (222) 308-2868.

Repeat the important info again and a phone number where they can call for tickets.

Photo: Lyn Walker and Roger Ebell star in PROOF.

I always recommend supplying a photo. It gives you a better shot at getting it printed. Include a photo tag naming the people in the photo.

CONTACT: Lyn Walker (212) 222-2222

Always put a contact number to reach ☞
you for more information.

Correspondence

Keep track of all your correspondence and submissions to agents,
casting directors, directors, etc. Label your photos, reels and demos
P1, P2, P3, R1, R2, D1, D2, etc. to track which one gets the best
response. Use the $ column for postage costs and transfer them at
the end of the year to your Marketing Expenses section.

Date	Who	Regarding	Sent	Result	$
5/1	Telsey	IBM Industrial Video	R1/P1	got appt.	2.50
5/5	Jay Binder	Billy in 42nd Street	P2	none	60¢
		TOTAL POSTAGE			
		BEST TOOL			

Correspondence

Date	Who	Regarding	Sent	Result	$
			TOTAL POSTAGE		
			BEST TOOL		

Correspondence

Date	Who	Regarding	Sent	Result	$
			TOTAL POSTAGE		
			BEST TOOL		

Correspondence

Date	Who	Regarding	Sent	Result	$
		TOTAL POSTAGE			
		BEST TOOL			

Correspondence

Date	Who	Regarding	Sent	Result	$
		TOTAL POSTAGE			
		BEST TOOL			

Correspondence

Date	Who	Regarding	Sent	Result	$
		TOTAL POSTAGE			
		TOTAL POSTAGE ALL PAGES			
		BEST TOOL			

Audition Log

Tracking Your Progress

Working is what the actor strives for! Getting paid to do what you love is the ultimate reward! Anything worthwhile is worth working for. And for actors, the joy of being in front of an audience, camera or microphone far outweighs the frustrations of looking for that next gig. Unfortunately, working is only a small part of being an actor. About 95% of being an actor is working at getting work. So, here's the section to keep track of all your "working at getting work" days.

Aside from going on auditions, here are several other ways to work at getting work everyday.

TRAINING: Improving your craft is an integral part of being an actor. You must work at it daily. Besides, you never know who you'll meet in class.

MARKETING: Commit to sending out something to market yourself on a specific schedule. Keep people interested all year round. Find something pertinent to write about such as upcoming projects, reviews you got from your last job or other information that may spark them bring you in for an audition or offer you a job.

DIRECTORS: Pick up the phone and call a director you enjoyed working with and simply say hello and find out what he/she is working on. It's not a call to bug them for work...it's a business call with a personal touch. Be sure you have something to say before picking up the phone.

WRITERS: Get to know playwrights and composers so you can get in on the ground level of new works. Volunteer your time as a reader or singer in a writers workshop.

Audition Info

Project Title	Role
Wicked	Elphaba

Casting Director	Medium
Bernard Telsey	Broadway

Audition Date	Time	Submitted By
February 3	4:30	ICM

Audition Location
Chelsea Studios

Materials to Prepare
Defying Gravity and Sides

Producing Company
Universal

Director	Assistant Director
Joe Mantello	~~SAMPLE~~

Music Director
Stephen Oremus

People in Audition Room
Stephen, Joe, Bernard, Kelli (assistant)

Materials Presented
Defying Gravity, sides, Wizard and I

Wardrobe
Black dress with black turtleneck

Comments
Sang great! My read could have been bet
ter. They called me back though

FARE/GAS.	PARKING	CALLED BACK	THANK YOU	BOOKED
$4		X	X	

Audition Info

Project Title   Role

Casting Director   Medium

Audition Date   Time   Submitted By

Audition Location

Materials to Prepare

Producing Company

Director   Assistant Director

Music Director   Choreographer

People in Audition Room

Materials Presented

Wardrobe

Comments

FARE/GAS.	PARKING	CALLED BACK	THANK YOU	BOOKED

Audition Info

Project Title	**Role**

Casting Director	**Medium**

Audition Date	**Time**	**Submitted By**

Audition Location

Materials to Prepare

Producing Company

Director	**Assistant Director**

Music Director	**Choreographer**

People in Audition Room

Materials Presented

Wardrobe

Comments

FARE/GAS.	PARKING	CALLED BACK	THANK YOU	BOOKED

Audition Info

Project Title Role

Casting Director Medium

Audition Date Time Submitted By

Audition Location

Materials to Prepare

Producing Company

Director Assistant Director

Music Director Choreographer

People in Audition Room

Materials Presented

Wardrobe

Comments

FARE/GAS.	PARKING	CALLED BACK	THANK YOU	BOOKED

Audition Info

Project Title	Role

Casting Director	Medium

Audition Date	Time	Submitted By

Audition Location

Materials to Prepare

Producing Company

Director	Assistant Director

Music Director	Choreographer

People in Audition Room

Materials Presented

Wardrobe

Comments

FARE/GAS.	PARKING	CALLED BACK	THANK YOU	BOOKED

Audition Info

Project Title	**Role**
Casting Director	**Medium**
Audition Date	**Time** **Submitted By**
Audition Location	
Materials to Prepare	
Producing Company	
Director	**Assistant Director**
Music Director	**Choreographer**
People in Audition Room	
Materials Presented	
Wardrobe	
Comments	

FARE/GAS.	PARKING	CALLED BACK	THANK YOU	BOOKED

Audition Info

Project Title	**Role**

Casting Director	**Medium**

Audition Date	**Time**	**Submitted By**

Audition Location

Materials to Prepare

Producing Company

Director	**Assistant Director**

Music Director	**Choreographer**

People in Audition Room

Materials Presented

Wardrobe

Comments

FARE/GAS.	PARKING	CALLED BACK	THANK YOU	BOOKED

Audition Info

Project Title	**Role**
Casting Director	**Medium**
Audition Date	**Time** **Submitted By**
Audition Location	
Materials to Prepare	
Producing Company	
Director	**Assistant Director**
Music Director	**Choreographer**
People in Audition Room	
Materials Presented	
Wardrobe	
Comments	

FARE/GAS.	PARKING	CALLED BACK	THANK YOU	BOOKED

Audition Info

Project Title	**Role**
Casting Director	**Medium**
Audition Date	**Time** **Submitted By**
Audition Location	
Materials to Prepare	
Producing Company	
Director	**Assistant Director**
Music Director	**Choreographer**
People in Audition Room	
Materials Presented	
Wardrobe	
Comments	

FARE/GAS.	PARKING	CALLED BACK	THANK YOU	BOOKED

Audition Info

Project Title	**Role**

Casting Director	**Medium**

Audition Date	**Time**	**Submitted By**

Audition Location

Materials to Prepare

Producing Company

Director	**Assistant Director**

Music Director	**Choreographer**

People in Audition Room

Materials Presented

Wardrobe

Comments

FARE/GAS.	PARKING	CALLED BACK	THANK YOU	BOOKED

Audition Info

Project Title	Role	

Casting Director	Medium	

Audition Date	Time	Submitted By

Audition Location

Materials to Prepare

Producing Company

Director	Assistant Director

Music Director	Choreographer

People in Audition Room

Materials Presented

Wardrobe

Comments

FARE/GAS.	PARKING	CALLED BACK	THANK YOU	BOOKED

Audition Info

Project Title	**Role**
Casting Director	**Medium**
Audition Date	**Time** **Submitted By**
Audition Location	
Materials to Prepare	
Producing Company	
Director	**Assistant Director**
Music Director	**Choreographer**
People in Audition Room	
Materials Presented	
Wardrobe	
Comments	

FARE/GAS.	PARKING	CALLED BACK	THANK YOU	BOOKED

Audition Info

Project Title	**Role**
Casting Director	**Medium**
Audition Date	**Time** **Submitted By**
Audition Location	
Materials to Prepare	
Producing Company	
Director	**Assistant Director**
Music Director	**Choreographer**
People in Audition Room	
Materials Presented	
Wardrobe	
Comments	

FARE/GAS.	PARKING	CALLED BACK	THANK YOU	BOOKED

Audition Info

Project Title	**Role**
Casting Director	**Medium**
Audition Date	**Time** **Submitted By**
Audition Location	
Materials to Prepare	
Producing Company	
Director	**Assistant Director**
Music Director	**Choreographer**
People in Audition Room	
Materials Presented	
Wardrobe	
Comments	

FARE/GAS.	PARKING	CALLED BACK	THANK YOU	BOOKED

Audition Info

Project Title	**Role**
Casting Director	**Medium**
Audition Date	**Time** **Submitted By**
Audition Location	
Materials to Prepare	
Producing Company	
Director	**Assistant Director**
Music Director	**Choreographer**
People in Audition Room	
Materials Presented	
Wardrobe	
Comments	

FARE/GAS.	PARKING	CALLED BACK	THANK YOU	BOOKED

Audition Info

Project Title	**Role**

Casting Director	**Medium**

Audition Date	**Time**	**Submitted By**

Audition Location

Materials to Prepare

Producing Company

Director	**Assistant Director**

Music Director	**Choreographer**

People in Audition Room

Materials Presented

Wardrobe

Comments

FARE/GAS.	PARKING	CALLED BACK	THANK YOU	BOOKED

Audition Info

Project Title	**Role**
Casting Director	**Medium**
Audition Date	**Time** **Submitted By**
Audition Location	
Materials to Prepare	
Producing Company	
Director	**Assistant Director**
Music Director	**Choreographer**
People in Audition Room	
Materials Presented	
Wardrobe	
Comments	

FARE/GAS.	PARKING	CALLED BACK	THANK YOU	BOOKED

Audition Info

Project Title   Role

Casting Director   Medium

Audition Date   Time   Submitted By

Audition Location

Materials to Prepare

Producing Company

Director   Assistant Director

Music Director   Choreographer

People in Audition Room

_____

Materials Presented

Wardrobe

Comments

FARE/GAS.	PARKING	CALLED BACK	THANK YOU	BOOKED

Audition Info

Project Title	**Role**
Casting Director	**Medium**
Audition Date	**Time** **Submitted By**
Audition Location	
Materials to Prepare	
Producing Company	
Director	**Assistant Director**
Music Director	**Choreographer**
People in Audition Room	
Materials Presented	
Wardrobe	
Comments	

FARE/GAS.	PARKING	CALLED BACK	THANK YOU	BOOKED

Audition Info

Project Title	Role	

Casting Director	Medium	

Audition Date	Time	Submitted By

Audition Location

Materials to Prepare

Producing Company

Director	Assistant Director

Music Director	Choreographer

People in Audition Room

Materials Presented

Wardrobe

Comments

FARE/GAS.	PARKING	CALLED BACK	THANK YOU	BOOKED

Audition Info

Project Title	**Role**
Casting Director	**Medium**
Audition Date	**Time** **Submitted By**
Audition Location	
Materials to Prepare	
Producing Company	
Director	**Assistant Director**
Music Director	**Choreographer**
People in Audition Room	
Materials Presented	
Wardrobe	
Comments	

FARE/GAS.	PARKING	CALLED BACK	THANK YOU	BOOKED

Audition Info

Project Title	**Role**
Casting Director	**Medium**
Audition Date	**Time** **Submitted By**
Audition Location	
Materials to Prepare	
Producing Company	
Director	**Assistant Director**
Music Director	**Choreographer**
People in Audition Room	
Materials Presented	
Wardrobe	
Comments	

FARE/GAS.	PARKING	CALLED BACK	THANK YOU	BOOKED

Audition Info

Project Title	**Role**
Casting Director	**Medium**
Audition Date	**Time** **Submitted By**
Audition Location	
Materials to Prepare	
Producing Company	
Director	**Assistant Director**
Music Director	**Choreographer**
People in Audition Room	
Materials Presented	
Wardrobe	
Comments	

FARE/GAS.	PARKING	CALLED BACK	THANK YOU	BOOKED

Audition Info

Project Title   Role

Casting Director   Medium

Audition Date   Time   Submitted By

Audition Location

Materials to Prepare

Producing Company

Director   Assistant Director

Music Director   Choreographer

People in Audition Room

Materials Presented

Wardrobe

Comments

FARE/GAS.	PARKING	CALLED BACK	THANK YOU	BOOKED

Audition Info

Project Title	Role
Casting Director	Medium
Audition Date	Time Submitted By
Audition Location	
Materials to Prepare	

Producing Company

Director	Assistant Director
Music Director	Choreographer

People in Audition Room

Materials Presented

Wardrobe

Comments

FARE/GAS.	PARKING	CALLED BACK	THANK YOU	BOOKED

Audition Info

Project Title	**Role**
Casting Director	**Medium**
Audition Date	**Time** **Submitted By**
Audition Location	
Materials to Prepare	
Producing Company	
Director	**Assistant Director**
Music Director	**Choreographer**
People in Audition Room	
Materials Presented	
Wardrobe	
Comments	

FARE/GAS.	PARKING	**CALLED BACK**	**THANK YOU**	**BOOKED**

Audition Info

Project Title	**Role**

Casting Director	**Medium**

Audition Date	**Time**	**Submitted By**

Audition Location

Materials to Prepare

Producing Company

Director	**Assistant Director**

Music Director	**Choreographer**

People in Audition Room

Materials Presented

Wardrobe

Comments

FARE/GAS.	PARKING	CALLED BACK	THANK YOU	BOOKED

Audition Info

Project Title	**Role**
Casting Director	**Medium**
Audition Date	**Time** **Submitted By**

Audition Location

Materials to Prepare

Producing Company

Director	**Assistant Director**
Music Director	**Choreographer**

People in Audition Room

Materials Presented

Wardrobe

Comments

FARE/GAS.	PARKING	CALLED BACK	THANK YOU	BOOKED

Audition Info

Project Title	**Role**
Casting Director	**Medium**
Audition Date	**Time** **Submitted By**
Audition Location	
Materials to Prepare	

Producing Company

Director	**Assistant Director**
Music Director	**Choreographer**

People in Audition Room

Materials Presented

Wardrobe

Comments

FARE/GAS.	PARKING	CALLED BACK	THANK YOU	BOOKED

Audition Info

Project Title	**Role**
Casting Director	**Medium**
Audition Date	**Time** **Submitted By**
Audition Location	
Materials to Prepare	
Producing Company	
Director	**Assistant Director**
Music Director	**Choreographer**

People in Audition Room

Materials Presented

Wardrobe

Comments

FARE/GAS.	PARKING	CALLED BACK	THANK YOU	BOOKED

Audition Info

Project Title	**Role**
Casting Director	**Medium**
Audition Date	**Time** **Submitted By**
Audition Location	
Materials to Prepare	
Producing Company	
Director	**Assistant Director**
Music Director	**Choreographer**
People in Audition Room	
Materials Presented	
Wardrobe	
Comments	

FARE/GAS.	PARKING	CALLED BACK	THANK YOU	BOOKED

Audition Info

Project Title   **Role**

Casting Director   **Medium**

Audition Date   **Time**   **Submitted By**

Audition Location

Materials to Prepare

Producing Company

Director   **Assistant Director**

Music Director   **Choreographer**

People in Audition Room

Materials Presented

Wardrobe

Comments

FARE/GAS.	PARKING	CALLED BACK	THANK YOU	BOOKED

Audition Info

Project Title	**Role**
Casting Director	**Medium**
Audition Date	**Time** **Submitted By**
Audition Location	
Materials to Prepare	
Producing Company	
Director	**Assistant Director**
Music Director	**Choreographer**
People in Audition Room	
Materials Presented	
Wardrobe	
Comments	

FARE/GAS.	PARKING	CALLED BACK	THANK YOU	BOOKED

Audition Info

Project Title	**Role**
Casting Director	**Medium**
Audition Date	**Time** **Submitted By**
Audition Location	
Materials to Prepare	
Producing Company	
Director	**Assistant Director**
Music Director	**Choreographer**
People in Audition Room	
Materials Presented	
Wardrobe	
Comments	

FARE/GAS.	PARKING	CALLED BACK	THANK YOU	BOOKED

Audition Info

Project Title	**Role**
Casting Director	**Medium**
Audition Date	**Time** **Submitted By**
Audition Location	
Materials to Prepare	
Producing Company	
Director	**Assistant Director**
Music Director	**Choreographer**

People in Audition Room

Materials Presented

Wardrobe

Comments

FARE/GAS.	PARKING	CALLED BACK	THANK YOU	BOOKED

Audition Info

Project Title	**Role**
Casting Director	**Medium**
Audition Date	**Time** **Submitted By**
Audition Location	
Materials to Prepare	
Producing Company	
Director	**Assistant Director**
Music Director	**Choreographer**

People in Audition Room

Materials Presented

Wardrobe

Comments

FARE/GAS.	PARKING	CALLED BACK	THANK YOU	BOOKED

Audition Info

Project Title	**Role**
Casting Director	**Medium**
Audition Date	**Time** **Submitted By**
Audition Location	
Materials to Prepare	
Producing Company	
Director	**Assistant Director**
Music Director	**Choreographer**
People in Audition Room	
Materials Presented	
Wardrobe	
Comments	

FARE/GAS.	PARKING	CALLED BACK	THANK YOU	BOOKED

Audition Info

Project Title   Role

Casting Director   Medium

Audition Date   Time   Submitted By

Audition Location

Materials to Prepare

Producing Company

Director   Assistant Director

Music Director   Choreographer

People in Audition Room

Materials Presented

Wardrobe

Comments

FARE/GAS.	PARKING	CALLED BACK	THANK YOU	BOOKED

Audition Info

Project Title	**Role**
Casting Director	**Medium**
Audition Date	**Time** **Submitted By**
Audition Location	
Materials to Prepare	
Producing Company	
Director	**Assistant Director**
Music Director	**Choreographer**
People in Audition Room	
Materials Presented	
Wardrobe	
Comments	

FARE/GAS.	PARKING	CALLED BACK	THANK YOU	BOOKED

Audition Info

Project Title	**Role**

Casting Director   **Medium**

Audition Date   **Time**   **Submitted By**

Audition Location

Materials to Prepare

Producing Company

Director   **Assistant Director**

Music Director   **Choreographer**

People in Audition Room

Materials Presented

Wardrobe

Comments

FARE/GAS.	PARKING	CALLED BACK	THANK YOU	BOOKED

Audition Info

Project Title	**Role**
Casting Director	**Medium**
Audition Date	**Time**　　**Submitted By**
Audition Location	
Materials to Prepare	
Producing Company	
Director	**Assistant Director**
Music Director	**Choreographer**
People in Audition Room	
Materials Presented	
Wardrobe	
Comments	

FARE/GAS.	PARKING	CALLED BACK	THANK YOU	BOOKED

Audition Info

Project Title	**Role**
Casting Director	**Medium**
Audition Date	**Time** **Submitted By**
Audition Location	
Materials to Prepare	
Producing Company	
Director	**Assistant Director**
Music Director	**Choreographer**
People in Audition Room	
Materials Presented	
Wardrobe	
Comments	

FARE/GAS.	PARKING	CALLED BACK	THANK YOU	BOOKED

Audition Info

Project Title	**Role**

Casting Director	**Medium**

Audition Date	**Time**	**Submitted By**

Audition Location

Materials to Prepare

Producing Company

Director	**Assistant Director**

Music Director	**Choreographer**

People in Audition Room

Materials Presented

Wardrobe

Comments

FARE/GAS.	PARKING	CALLED BACK	THANK YOU	BOOKED

Audition Info

Project Title	**Role**
Casting Director	**Medium**
Audition Date	**Time**　　**Submitted By**
Audition Location	
Materials to Prepare	
Producing Company	
Director	**Assistant Director**
Music Director	**Choreographer**
People in Audition Room	
Materials Presented	
Wardrobe	
Comments	

FARE/GAS.	PARKING	CALLED BACK	THANK YOU	BOOKED

Audition Info

Project Title	Role	
Casting Director	Medium	
Audition Date	Time	Submitted By
Audition Location		
Materials to Prepare		
Producing Company		
Director	Assistant Director	
Music Director	Choreographer	
People in Audition Room		
Materials Presented		
Wardrobe		
Comments		

FARE/GAS.	PARKING	CALLED BACK	THANK YOU	BOOKED

Audition Info

Project Title	**Role**
Casting Director	**Medium**
Audition Date	**Time** **Submitted By**
Audition Location	
Materials to Prepare	
Producing Company	
Director	**Assistant Director**
Music Director	**Choreographer**
People in Audition Room	
Materials Presented	
Wardrobe	
Comments	

FARE/GAS.	PARKING	CALLED BACK	THANK YOU	BOOKED

Audition Info

Project Title	**Role**	
Casting Director	**Medium**	
Audition Date	**Time**	**Submitted By**
Audition Location		
Materials to Prepare		
Producing Company		
Director	**Assistant Director**	
Music Director	**Choreographer**	
People in Audition Room		
Materials Presented		
Wardrobe		
Comments		

FARE/GAS.	PARKING	CALLED BACK	THANK YOU	BOOKED

Audition Info

Project Title	Role
Casting Director	Medium
Audition Date	Time	Submitted By
Audition Location	
Materials to Prepare	
Producing Company	
Director	Assistant Director
Music Director	Choreographer
People in Audition Room	
Materials Presented	
Wardrobe	
Comments	

FARE/GAS.	PARKING	CALLED BACK	THANK YOU	BOOKED

Audition Info

Project Title	**Role**
Casting Director	**Medium**
Audition Date	**Time** **Submitted By**
Audition Location	
Materials to Prepare	
Producing Company	
Director	**Assistant Director**
Music Director	**Choreographer**
People in Audition Room	
Materials Presented	
Wardrobe	
Comments	

FARE/GAS.	PARKING	CALLED BACK	THANK YOU	BOOKED

Audition Info

Project Title	**Role**
Casting Director	**Medium**
Audition Date	**Time** **Submitted By**
Audition Location	
Materials to Prepare	
Producing Company	
Director	**Assistant Director**
Music Director	**Choreographer**
People in Audition Room	

Materials Presented

Wardrobe

Comments

FARE/GAS.	PARKING	CALLED BACK	THANK YOU	BOOKED

Audition Info

Project Title	**Role**

Casting Director	**Medium**

Audition Date	**Time**	**Submitted By**

Audition Location

Materials to Prepare

Producing Company

Director	**Assistant Director**

Music Director	**Choreographer**

People in Audition Room

Materials Presented

Wardrobe

Comments

FARE/GAS.	PARKING	CALLED BACK	THANK YOU	BOOKED

Audition Info

Project Title	**Role**
Casting Director	**Medium**
Audition Date	**Time** **Submitted By**
Audition Location	
Materials to Prepare	
Producing Company	
Director	**Assistant Director**
Music Director	**Choreographer**
People in Audition Room	
Materials Presented	
Wardrobe	
Comments	

FARE/GAS.	PARKING	CALLED BACK	THANK YOU	BOOKED

Audition Info

Project Title	**Role**
Casting Director	**Medium**
Audition Date	**Time** **Submitted By**
Audition Location	
Materials to Prepare	
Producing Company	
Director	**Assistant Director**
Music Director	**Choreographer**
People in Audition Room	
Materials Presented	
Wardrobe	
Comments	

FARE/GAS.	PARKING	CALLED BACK	THANK YOU	BOOKED

Audition Info

Project Title   **Role**

Casting Director   **Medium**

Audition Date   **Time**   **Submitted By**

Audition Location

Materials to Prepare

Producing Company

Director   **Assistant Director**

Music Director   **Choreographer**

People in Audition Room

Materials Presented

Wardrobe

Comments

FARE/GAS.	PARKING	CALLED BACK	THANK YOU	BOOKED

Audition Info

Project Title	**Role**
Casting Director	**Medium**
Audition Date	**Time** **Submitted By**
Audition Location	
Materials to Prepare	
Producing Company	
Director	**Assistant Director**
Music Director	**Choreographer**
People in Audition Room	
Materials Presented	
Wardrobe	
Comments	

FARE/GAS.	PARKING	CALLED BACK	THANK YOU	BOOKED

Audition Info

Project Title	**Role**
Casting Director	**Medium**
Audition Date	**Time** **Submitted By**
Audition Location	
Materials to Prepare	
Producing Company	
Director	**Assistant Director**
Music Director	**Choreographer**
People in Audition Room	
Materials Presented	
Wardrobe	
Comments	

FARE/GAS.	PARKING	CALLED BACK	THANK YOU	BOOKED

Audition Info

Project Title	**Role**
Casting Director	**Medium**
Audition Date	**Time** **Submitted By**
Audition Location	
Materials to Prepare	
Producing Company	
Director	**Assistant Director**
Music Director	**Choreographer**
People in Audition Room	
Materials Presented	
Wardrobe	
Comments	

FARE/GAS.	PARKING	CALLED BACK	THANK YOU	BOOKED

Audition Info

Project Title   Role

Casting Director   Medium

Audition Date   Time   Submitted By

Audition Location

Materials to Prepare

Producing Company

Director   Assistant Director

Music Director   Choreographer

People in Audition Room

Materials Presented

Wardrobe

Comments

FARE/GAS.	PARKING	CALLED BACK	THANK YOU	BOOKED

Audition Info

Project Title	**Role**

Casting Director	**Medium**

Audition Date	**Time**	**Submitted By**

Audition Location

Materials to Prepare

Producing Company

Director	**Assistant Director**

Music Director	**Choreographer**

People in Audition Room

Materials Presented

Wardrobe

Comments

FARE/GAS.	PARKING	CALLED BACK	THANK YOU	BOOKED

Audition Info

Project Title	Role	

Casting Director	Medium	

Audition Date	Time	Submitted By

Audition Location

Materials to Prepare

Producing Company

Director	Assistant Director

Music Director	Choreographer

People in Audition Room

Materials Presented

Wardrobe

Comments

FARE/GAS.	PARKING	CALLED BACK	THANK YOU	BOOKED

Finances

Knowing Where Your Money Goes

The financial aspects of having an acting career can be overwhelming. Top level jobs in show business can be extremely lucrative. Unfortunately, sometimes it takes an actor quite a long time to get to the high paying jobs and even then it doesn't mean he will continue to make that money consistently. So budgeting and tracking your expenses is crucial. Along with you being the CEO of your business, you also need to be the CFO (Chief Financial Officer) which means you've got to create a workable budget and track your income and expenses.

I know, I know...you didn't get into acting to be an accountant, but guess what? It's part of your business and therefore you must take responsibility for it. Of particular importance for your taxes are your expenses. Most everything you use as an actor to promote yourself is tax deductible, including this book!

I do not pretend to be a tax specialist. Nor do I promote the following pages as the only way to keep track of expenses. I do know it is crucial to document everything. If you are not proficient at your own taxes, I would recommend getting professional assistance. (If you are a member of Actors Equity Association, you can get them done for free through the union. But be sure to sign up early).

I encourage you to keep track of your expenses as they accrue. It's much more difficult to go back at the end of the year and try to remember what all your bills were. And, just because you wrote it down here does not mean that you don't need a receipt to back it up. A credit card statement is not enough! YOU MUST KEEP ALL OF YOUR RECEIPTS AND BILLS FOR TAX PURPOSES. If the receipt is not self-explanatory, be sure to write down any pertinent information on the back of it.

Projected Budget

Decide how much you want to spend on your career and how much you'd like to make. Compare it to actual totals at the end of the year.

	jan	feb	mar	apr	may	june	july	aug	sept	oct	nov	dec
EXPENSE												
training												
marketing												
research												
travel												
industry												
image												
phone												
PROJECTED TOTAL												
ACTUAL TOTAL												
PROJECTED INCOME												
ACTUAL INCOME												

Income

Record income from your industry related jobs. I've added columns to tabulate your 401k contributions, commissions paid and dues.

date	source	salary	per diem	commission paid	per diem	dues paid	401K contribute	NET PAY

Income

Record income from your industry related jobs. I've added columns to tabulate your 401k contributions, commissions paid and dues.

date	source	salary	per diem	commission paid	dues paid	401K contribute	NET PAY

Income

Record income from your industry related jobs. I've added columns to tabulate your 401k contributions, commissions paid and dues.

date	source	salary	per diem	commission paid	dues paid	401K contribute	NET PAY

Training Expenses

Record expenses for classes, private coachings, seminars, workshops, etc.
Use the boxes for how you paid $=cash, √=check CH=charge.
For private coachings have your teacher write the cost on the back of their business card after each session.

Date	Item Description	Cost	$	√	CH

Date	Item Description	Cost	$	√	CH
	Total				

Marketing Expenses

Record expenses for photos, resumes, postcards, fliers, reels, tapes, etc.
Use the boxes for how you paid $=cash, √=check CH=charge.
The postage total is carried over from your correspondence page.

Date	Item Description	Cost	$	√	CH

Date	Item Description	Cost	$	√	CH
	Postage Total(From Correspondence)				
	GRAND TOTAL				

Travel Expenses

Record all of your travel expenses including airfare, parking, tolls, trains, subways, buses, hotels, etc. as they pertain to your career. You can not write off reimbursed travel costs. Ask your accountant about per diem checks and how to document use.

Date	Description of Travel	Cost

Date	Description of Travel	Cost
	Total Travel	
	Total Audition Travel (from Audition Log)	
	Grand Total	

Research Expenses

Record expenses for show tickets, books, scripts, CD's, video rentals, etc.
Use the boxes for how you paid $=cash, √=check CH=charge.
*Keep in mind there's a fine line between research and entertainment.

Date	Item Description	Cost	$	√	CH

Date	Item Description	Cost	$	√	CH
	Total				

Communication Expenses

Record expenses for phones, voicemail, internet, etc.
Use the boxes for what type of bill P=phone C=cell I=Internet V=voicemail or describe other.
*With home phones you can only write off business calls.

Month	Amount	P	C	I	V	Other

Month	Amount		P	C	I	V	Other
Total							

Industry Expenses

Record expenses for dues, trade publications, professional memberships, backstage tips, etc.
Use the boxes for how you paid $=cash, √=check CH=charge.

Date	Item Description	Cost	$	√	CH

Date	Item Description	Cost	$	√	CH
	Dues Deducted from Pay				
	Commissions Paid				
	Total				

Image Expenses

Record expenses for audition wardrobe, show make up, hair cuts, etc.
Use the boxes for how you paid $=cash, √=check CH=charge.
*Keep in mind this is an iffy category, so be sure to ask your accountant.

Date	Item Description	Cost	$	√	CH
	Total				

Miscellaneous Expenses

Record expenses for other stuff you use for your career.
Use the boxes for how you paid $=cash, √=check CH=charge.
*You must document the necessity if not self explanatory.

Date	Item Description	Cost	$	√	CH
	Total				

Year-End Totals

Write in your expense totals for each category. This page can serve as the expense document you give your accountant at the end of the year. But don't forget to save all receipts too!

Category	Amount
TOTAL INCOME (from income pages)	
TRAINING EXPENSES	
MARKETING EXPENSES	
RESEARCH EXPENSES	
COMMUNICATION EXPENSES	
INDUSTRY EXPENSES	
TRAVEL EXPENSES	
IMAGE EXPENSES	
MISCELLANEOUS EXPENSES	
TOTAL EXPENSES	
NET INCOME (Income - Expenses)	

Industry Contacts

Keeping Your Industry Contacts In Order

We live in such an electronic world that nowadays we don't know anyone's phone number because we program them into our cell phones or PDA's. Of course if that electronic wizard dies or gets lost, all our numbers go with it. It may be easy to track down your friend's phone number, but it might be a bit harder to rebuild your valuable industry contacts. So, here's a great place to store all those really important numbers for your career. I've categorized them alphabetically by category for easy access.

You'll still need your PDA or computer for your big industry database (hopefully you're building one!). But, here, you can keep the ones you use the most.

I've also included a new page of useful phone numbers.

After inputting your new contacts, I suggest photocopying the pages or if you have a PDA, inputting them in there too. Then if you ever lose your Organized Actor®, you will have a record of your contacts. Doing this every three months or so will keep you current!

Numbers You Might Need

AIRLINES

AirTran	800-AIR-TRAN
American Airlines	800-433-7300
American Trans Air (ATA)	800-225-2995
America West	800-238-9292
Continental	800-525-0280
Delta/Song	800-221-1212
Frontier	800-432-1359
JetBlue	800-538-2583
NorthWest	800-225-2525
SouthWest	800-435-9792
United	800-241-6522
US Airways	800-428-4322

UNIONS

Actors Equity Association (NY)	212-869-8530
Actors Equity Association (LA)	323-634-1750
Actors Equity Association (Chicago)	312-641-0393
Pension and Health	212-869-9380
Screen Actors Guild (LA)	323-954-1600
Screen Actors Guild (NY)	212-944-1030
AFTRA (NY)	212-532-0800
AFTRA (LA)	323-634-8100

ORGANIZATIONS

Actor's Fund (National headquarters)	212-221-7300
Volunteer Lawyers for the Arts	212-319-ARTS ext 1
Performing Arts Library (NY)	212-870-1630

WEBSITES YOU SHOULD CHECK REGULARLY

organizedactor.com
playbill.com
actorsaccess.com
actorsequity.org
theatremania.com
broadway.com
broadwaystars.com
actorslife.com
sag.org
ibdb.com

Accompanists

Acting Teachers	

Casting Directors

Choreographers and Directors

Family and Friends

Music Directors

Photographers and Printers

Producers

Rehearsal Studios	

Theatre Companies

Voice Teachers

Other Contacts	

Calendar

Organizing Your Busy Schedule

Of all the new additions in this version of **The Organized Actor®**, this newly designed calendar section is my favorite! Now you can enjoy two full pages per week with designated time scheduling! But that's not all! You can also create a task list for each day and enjoy tallying up how many auditions, callbacks and meetings you had for the week so you get a feel for how aggressively you are pursuing your acting career. And don't worry, this new calendar is still good for a full year beginning from the date you purchase your book.

This new system is a powerful tool to help you accomplish more in your day and move forward quickly to attain your goals. Each week includes an inspirational quote or story that is sure to inspire you to reach for your dreams!

I've also included a yearly planning calendar to get an overall view of where you'll be during the year.

This new format, which I've been using myself for the last three months, has nearly doubled my productivity AND it has replaced all of my electronic calendars for efficiency. Now you only need this ONE CALENDAR for scheduling everything for your career and your life. Even if you're tied to your PDA, I challenge you try this system for three months!

For even better organization, purchase our customized tabs so you can find everything you're looking for in your Organized Actor® quickly and efficiently. Visit our website at www.OrganizedActor.com to purchase our tabs.

Enjoy getting organized!

Week of_____

MONDAY	TUESDAY	WEDNESDAY
8am	8am	8am
10	10	10
12	12	12
2	2	2
4	4	4
6	6	6
8pm	8pm	8pm
TO DO	TO DO	TO DO

"To lead a symphony, you must sometimes turn your back on the crowd."

THURSDAY		FRIDAY		SATURDAY	
8am		8am			
10		10			
12		12			
				SUNDAY	
2		2			
4		4			
6		6			
8pm		8pm		**WEEKLY TALLIES**	
				AUDITIONS	
				CALLBACKS	
TO DO		**TO DO**		MEETINGS	
				SEMINARS	
				CLASSES	
				PR'S SENT	
				FOLLOWUPS	

Week of_____

MONDAY	TUESDAY	WEDNESDAY
8am	8am	8am
10	10	10
12	12	12
2	2	2
4	4	4
6	6	6
8pm	8pm	8pm
TO DO	TO DO	TO DO

"To lead a symphony, you must sometimes turn your back on the crowd."

THURSDAY		FRIDAY		SATURDAY	
8am		8am			
10		10			
12		12			
				SUNDAY	
2		2			
4		4			
6		6			
8pm		8pm		**WEEKLY TALLIES**	
				AUDITIONS	
				CALLBACKS	
TO DO		TO DO		MEETINGS	
				SEMINARS	
				CLASSES	
				PR'S SENT	
				FOLLOWUPS	

Week of_____

MONDAY	TUESDAY	WEDNESDAY
8am	8am	8am
10	10	10
12	12	12
2	2	2
4	4	4
6	6	6
8pm	8pm	8pm
TO DO	TO DO	TO DO

"Success is a journey, not a destination."

THURSDAY		FRIDAY		SATURDAY	
8am		8am			
10		10			
12		12			
2		2		**SUNDAY**	
4		4			
6		6			
8pm		8pm		**WEEKLY TALLIES**	
TO DO		**TO DO**		AUDITIONS	
				CALLBACKS	
				MEETINGS	
				SEMINARS	
				CLASSES	
				PR'S SENT	
				FOLLOWUPS	

Week of_____

MONDAY	TUESDAY	WEDNESDAY
8am	8am	8am
10	10	10
12	12	12
2	2	2
4	4	4
6	6	6
8pm	8pm	8pm
TO DO	TO DO	TO DO

"Live with a feeling of gratitude for all the wealth you have in your life already."

THURSDAY		FRIDAY		SATURDAY	
8am		8am			
10		10			
12		12			
				SUNDAY	
2		2			
4		4			
6		6			
8pm		8pm		**WEEKLY TALLIES**	
				AUDITIONS	
				CALLBACKS	
TO DO		TO DO		MEETINGS	
				SEMINARS	
				CLASSES	
				PR'S SENT	
				FOLLOWUPS	

Week of_____

MONDAY	TUESDAY	WEDNESDAY
8am	8am	8am
10	10	10
12	12	12
2	2	2
4	4	4
6	6	6
8pm	8pm	8pm
TO DO	TO DO	TO DO

"Do what you love and the money will come."

THURSDAY		FRIDAY		SATURDAY	
8am		8am			
10		10			
12		12			
				SUNDAY	
2		2			
4		4			
6		6			
8pm		8pm		**WEEKLY TALLIES**	
TO DO		**TO DO**		AUDITIONS	
				CALLBACKS	
				MEETINGS	
				SEMINARS	
				CLASSES	
				PR'S SENT	
				FOLLOWUPS	

Week of_____

MONDAY		TUESDAY		WEDNESDAY	
8am		8am		8am	
10		10		10	
12		12		12	
2		2		2	
4		4		4	
6		6		6	
8pm		8pm		8pm	
TO DO		TO DO		TO DO	

"Think highly enough of yourself to NOT let your ego get in the way."

THURSDAY		FRIDAY		SATURDAY	
8am		8am			
10		10			
12		12			
				SUNDAY	
2		2			
4		4			
6		6			
8pm		8pm		**WEEKLY TALLIES**	
				AUDITIONS	
				CALLBACKS	
TO DO		**TO DO**		MEETINGS	
				SEMINARS	
				CLASSES	
				PR'S SENT	
				FOLLOWUPS	

Week of_____

MONDAY	TUESDAY	WEDNESDAY
8am	8am	8am
10	10	10
12	12	12
2	2	2
4	4	4
6	6	6
8pm	8pm	8pm
TO DO	TO DO	TO DO

"Do what's right."

THURSDAY		FRIDAY		SATURDAY	

THURSDAY | **FRIDAY** | **SATURDAY**

8am

10

12

2

4

6

8pm

TO DO

8am

10

12

2

4

6

8pm

TO DO

SUNDAY

WEEKLY TALLIES

AUDITIONS

CALLBACKS

MEETINGS

SEMINARS

CLASSES

PR'S SENT

FOLLOWUPS

Week of_____

MONDAY		TUESDAY		WEDNESDAY	
8am		8am		8am	
10		10		10	
12		12		12	
2		2		2	
4		4		4	
6		6		6	
8pm		8pm		8pm	
TO DO		TO DO		TO DO	

"Commit to constant and never-ending improvement."

THURSDAY		FRIDAY		SATURDAY	
8am		8am			
10		10			
12		12			
				SUNDAY	
2		2			
4		4			
6		6			
8pm		8pm		**WEEKLY TALLIES**	
				AUDITIONS	
				CALLBACKS	
TO DO		**TO DO**		MEETINGS	
				SEMINARS	
				CLASSES	
				PR'S SENT	
				FOLLOWUPS	

Week of_____

MONDAY	TUESDAY	WEDNESDAY
8am	8am	8am
10	10	10
12	12	12
2	2	2
4	4	4
6	6	6
8pm	8pm	8pm
TO DO	TO DO	TO DO

"Treat others with ultimate respect."

THURSDAY		FRIDAY		SATURDAY	
8am		8am			
10		10			
12		12			
				SUNDAY	
2		2			
4		4			
6		6			
8pm		8pm		**WEEKLY TALLIES**	
				AUDITIONS	
				CALLBACKS	
TO DO		TO DO		MEETINGS	
				SEMINARS	
				CLASSES	
				PR'S SENT	
				FOLLOWUPS	

Week of_____

MONEDAY		TUESDAY		WEDNESDAY	
8am		8am		8am	
10		10		10	
12		12		12	
2		2		2	
4		4		4	
6		6		6	
8pm		8pm		8pm	
TO DO		TO DO		TO DO	

"Seek knowledge in every situation you are blessed to experience."

THURSDAY		FRIDAY		SATURDAY	
8am		8am			
10		10			
12		12			
				SUNDAY	
2		2			
4		4			
6		6			
8pm		8pm		**WEEKLY TALLIES**	
				AUDITIONS	
				CALLBACKS	
TO DO		**TO DO**		MEETINGS	
				SEMINARS	
				CLASSES	
				PR'S SENT	
				FOLLOWUPS	

Week of_____

MONDAY	TUESDAY	WEDNESDAY
8am	8am	8am
10	10	10
12	12	12
2	2	2
4	4	4
6	6	6
8pm	8pm	8pm
TO DO	TO DO	TO DO

"If you're not part of the solution, you're part of the problem."

THURSDAY		FRIDAY		SATURDAY	
8am		8am			
10		10			
12		12			
				SUNDAY	
2		2			
4		4			
6		6			
8pm		8pm		**WEEKLY TALLIES**	
				AUDITIONS	
				CALLBACKS	
TO DO		TO DO		MEETINGS	
				SEMINARS	
				CLASSES	
				PR'S SENT	
				FOLLOWUPS	

Week of_____

MONDAY		TUESDAY		WEDNESDAY	
8am		8am		8am	
10		10		10	
12		12		12	
2		2		2	
4		4		4	
6		6		6	
8pm		8pm		8pm	
TO DO		TO DO		TO DO	

"Dream in vivid color."

THURSDAY		FRIDAY		SATURDAY	

THURSDAY

8am

10

12

2

4

6

8pm

TO DO

FRIDAY

8am

10

12

2

4

6

8pm

TO DO

SATURDAY

SUNDAY

WEEKLY TALLIES

AUDITIONS

CALLBACKS

MEETINGS

SEMINARS

CLASSES

PR'S SENT

FOLLOWUPS

Week of_____

MONDAY	TUESDAY	WEDNESDAY
8am	8am	8am
10	10	10
12	12	12
2	2	2
4	4	4
6	6	6
8pm	8pm	8pm
TO DO	TO DO	TO DO

"Unhappiness comes from not knowing what you want, and killing yourself to get it."

THURSDAY		FRIDAY		SATURDAY	
8am		8am			
10		10			
12		12			
				SUNDAY	
2		2			
4		4			
6		6			
8pm		8pm		**WEEKLY TALLIES**	
				AUDITIONS	
				CALLBACKS	
TO DO		TO DO		MEETINGS	
				SEMINARS	
				CLASSES	
				PR'S SENT	
				FOLLOWUPS	

Week of_____

MONDAY		TUESDAY		WEDNESDAY	
8am		8am		8am	
10		10		10	
12		12		12	
2		2		2	
4		4		4	
6		6		6	
8pm		8pm		8pm	
TO DO		TO DO		TO DO	

"Courage is not the lack of fear, but the conquest of it."

THURSDAY		FRIDAY		SATURDAY	
8am		8am			
10		10			
12		12			
2		2		**SUNDAY**	
4		4			
6		6			
8pm		8pm		**WEEKLY TALLIES**	
TO DO		TO DO		AUDITIONS	
				CALLBACKS	
				MEETINGS	
				SEMINARS	
				CLASSES	
				PR'S SENT	
				FOLLOWUPS	

Week of_____

MONDAY	TUESDAY	WEDNESDAY
8am	8am	8am
10	10	10
12	12	12
2	2	2
4	4	4
6	6	6
8pm	8pm	8pm
TO DO	TO DO	TO DO

"It's never too late to be what you might have been."

THURSDAY		FRIDAY		SATURDAY	
8am		8am			
10		10			
12		12			
				SUNDAY	
2		2			
4		4			
6		6			
8pm		8pm		**WEEKLY TALLIES**	
				AUDITIONS	
				CALLBACKS	
TO DO		**TO DO**		MEETINGS	
				SEMINARS	
				CLASSES	
				PR'S SENT	
				FOLLOWUPS	

Week of_____

MONDAY		TUESDAY		WEDNESDAY	
8am		8am		8am	
10		10		10	
12		12		12	
2		2		2	
4		4		4	
6		6		6	
8pm		8pm		8pm	
TO DO		TO DO		TO DO	

"See more in others than they see in themselves."

THURSDAY	FRIDAY	SATURDAY
8am	8am	
10	10	
12	12	
		SUNDAY
2	2	
4	4	
6	6	
8pm	8pm	**WEEKLY TALLIES**
		AUDITIONS
		CALLBACKS
TO DO	TO DO	MEETINGS
		SEMINARS
		CLASSES
		PR'S SENT
		FOLLOWUPS

Week of_____

MONDAY	TUESDAY	WEDNESDAY
8am	8am	8am
10	10	10
12	12	12
2	2	2
4	4	4
6	6	6
8pm	8pm	8pm
TO DO	TO DO	TO DO

"Do it now."

THURSDAY		FRIDAY		SATURDAY	
8am		8am			
10		10			
12		12			
2		2		**SUNDAY**	
4		4			
6		6			
8pm		8pm		**WEEKLY TALLIES**	
				AUDITIONS	
				CALLBACKS	
TO DO		TO DO		MEETINGS	
				SEMINARS	
				CLASSES	
				PR'S SENT	
				FOLLOWUPS	

Week of_____

MONDAY		TUESDAY		WEDNESDAY	
8am		8am		8am	
10		10		10	
12		12		12	
2		2		2	
4		4		4	
6		6		6	
8pm		8pm		8pm	
TO DO		TO DO		TO DO	

"Smile, laugh and sing every single day."

THURSDAY		FRIDAY		SATURDAY	
8am		8am			
10		10			
12		12			
				SUNDAY	
2		2			
4		4			
6		6			
8pm		8pm		**WEEKLY TALLIES**	
				AUDITIONS	
				CALLBACKS	
TO DO		**TO DO**		MEETINGS	
				SEMINARS	
				CLASSES	
				PR'S SENT	
				FOLLOWUPS	

Week of_____

MONDAY	TUESDAY	WEDNESDAY
8am	8am	8am
10	10	10
12	12	12
2	2	2
4	4	4
6	6	6
8pm	8pm	8pm
TO DO	TO DO	TO DO

"Make that call."

THURSDAY	FRIDAY	SATURDAY
8am	8am	
10	10	
12	12	
		SUNDAY
2	2	
4	4	
6	6	
8pm	8pm	**WEEKLY TALLIES**

WEEKLY TALLIES

AUDITIONS ☐

CALLBACKS ☐

MEETINGS ☐

SEMINARS ☐

CLASSES ☐

PR'S SENT ☐

FOLLOWUPS ☐

TO DO

TO DO

Week of_____

MONDAY	TUESDAY	WEDNESDAY
8am	8am	8am
10	10	10
12	12	12
2	2	2
4	4	4
6	6	6
8pm	8pm	8pm
TO DO	TO DO	TO DO

"Take a deep breath before you speak."

THURSDAY		FRIDAY		SATURDAY	
8am		8am			
10		10			
12		12			
2		2		**SUNDAY**	
4		4			
6		6			
8pm		8pm		**WEEKLY TALLIES**	
TO DO		TO DO		AUDITIONS	
				CALLBACKS	
				MEETINGS	
				SEMINARS	
				CLASSES	
				PR'S SENT	
				FOLLOWUPS	

Week of_____

MONDAY	TUESDAY	WEDNESDAY
8am	8am	8am
10	10	10
12	12	12
2	2	2
4	4	4
6	6	6
8pm	8pm	8pm
TO DO	**TO DO**	**TO DO**

"Say thank you."

THURSDAY		FRIDAY		SATURDAY	
8am		8am			
10		10			
12		12			
2		2		**SUNDAY**	
4		4			
6		6			
8pm		8pm		**WEEKLY TALLIES**	
TO DO		**TO DO**		AUDITIONS	
				CALLBACKS	
				MEETINGS	
				SEMINARS	
				CLASSES	
				PR'S SENT	
				FOLLOWUPS	

Week of_____

MONDAY	TUESDAY	WEDNESDAY
8am	8am	8am
10	10	10
12	12	12
2	2	2
4	4	4
6	6	6
8pm	8pm	8pm
TO DO	**TO DO**	**TO DO**

"Call your parents and/or your siblings to tell them you love them."

THURSDAY		FRIDAY		SATURDAY	
8am		8am			
10		10			
12		12			
2		2		**SUNDAY**	
4		4			
6		6			
8pm		8pm		**WEEKLY TALLIES**	
				AUDITIONS	
				CALLBACKS	
TO DO		TO DO		MEETINGS	
				SEMINARS	
				CLASSES	
				PR'S SENT	
				FOLLOWUPS	

Week of_____

MONDAY	TUESDAY	WEDNESDAY
8am	8am	8am
10	10	10
12	12	12
2	2	2
4	4	4
6	6	6
8pm	8pm	8pm
TO DO	TO DO	TO DO

"Take a pottery or painting class."

THURSDAY		FRIDAY		SATURDAY	
8am		8am			
10		10			
12		12			
				SUNDAY	
2		2			
4		4			
6		6			
8pm		8pm		**WEEKLY TALLIES**	
				AUDITIONS	
				CALLBACKS	
TO DO		**TO DO**		MEETINGS	
				SEMINARS	
				CLASSES	
				PR'S SENT	
				FOLLOWUPS	

Week of_____

MONDAY	TUESDAY	WEDNESDAY
8am	8am	8am
10	10	10
12	12	12
2	2	2
4	4	4
6	6	6
8pm	8pm	8pm
TO DO	TO DO	TO DO

Yes, you can make a fabulous life as an actor!

THURSDAY	FRIDAY	SATURDAY
8am	8am	
10	10	
12	12	
		SUNDAY
2	2	
4	4	
6	6	
8pm	8pm	**WEEKLY TALLIES**

WEEKLY TALLIES

AUDITIONS

CALLBACKS

MEETINGS

SEMINARS

CLASSES

PR'S SENT

FOLLOWUPS

TO DO

TO DO

Week of_____

MONDAY	TUESDAY	WEDNESDAY
8am	8am	8am
10	10	10
12	12	12
2	2	2
4	4	4
6	6	6
8pm	8pm	8pm
TO DO	TO DO	TO DO

After Fred Astaire's first screen test, the memo from the testing director from MGM said, "Can't sing. Can't act. Can dance a little." Astaire kept that memo over the fireplace in his Beverly HIlls home.

THURSDAY	FRIDAY	SATURDAY
8am	8am	
10	10	
12	12	
2	2	**SUNDAY**
4	4	
6	6	
8pm	8pm	**WEEKLY TALLIES**

WEEKLY TALLIES

AUDITIONS

CALLBACKS

MEETINGS

SEMINARS

CLASSES

PR'S SENT

FOLLOWUPS

TO DO

TO DO

Week of_____

MONDAY	TUESDAY	WEDNESDAY
8am	8am	8am
10	10	10
12	12	12
2	2	2
4	4	4
6	6	6
8pm	8pm	8pm
TO DO	TO DO	TO DO

Beethoven's teacher called him hopeless as a composer.

THURSDAY		FRIDAY		SATURDAY	
8am		8am			
10		10			
12		12			
				SUNDAY	
2		2			
4		4			
6		6			
8pm		8pm		**WEEKLY TALLIES**	
				AUDITIONS	
				CALLBACKS	
TO DO		**TO DO**		MEETINGS	
				SEMINARS	
				CLASSES	
				PR'S SENT	
				FOLLOWUPS	

Week of_____

MONDAY	TUESDAY	WEDNESDAY
8am	8am	8am
10	10	10
12	12	12
2	2	2
4	4	4
6	6	6
8pm	8pm	8pm
TO DO	TO DO	TO DO

Barbara Streisand's mother said she could never be a star because she was too ugly.

THURSDAY	FRIDAY	SATURDAY
8am	8am	
10	10	
12	12	
		SUNDAY
2	2	
4	4	
6	6	
8pm	8pm	**WEEKLY TALLIES**
		AUDITIONS
		CALLBACKS
TO DO	**TO DO**	MEETINGS
		SEMINARS
		CLASSES
		PR'S SENT
		FOLLOWUPS

Week of_____

MONDAY		TUESDAY		WEDNESDAY	
8am		8am		8am	
10		10		10	
12		12		12	
2		2		2	
4		4		4	
6		6		6	
8pm		8pm		8pm	
TO DO		TO DO		TO DO	

Sylvester Stallone was turned down by over 200 agents when he wrote Rocky and wanted to star in it. Someone offered to produce it if he DIDN'T star in it. Well, we know what really happened.

THURSDAY		FRIDAY		SATURDAY	
8am		8am			
10		10			
12		12			
				SUNDAY	
2		2			
4		4			
6		6			
8pm		8pm		**WEEKLY TALLIES**	
				AUDITIONS	
				CALLBACKS	
TO DO		TO DO		MEETINGS	
				SEMINARS	
				CLASSES	
				PR'S SENT	
				FOLLOWUPS	

Week of_____

MONDAY	TUESDAY	WEDNESDAY
8am	8am	8am
10	10	10
12	12	12
2	2	2
4	4	4
6	6	6
8pm	8pm	8pm
TO DO	**TO DO**	**TO DO**

Walt Disney was fired by a newspaper for lack of ideas. And he was turned down by 70 banks to build Disneyland because they thought the idea would never work.

THURSDAY		FRIDAY		SATURDAY	
8am		8am			
10		10			
12		12			
2		2		**SUNDAY**	
4		4			
6		6			
8pm		8pm		**WEEKLY TALLIES**	
				AUDITIONS	
				CALLBACKS	
TO DO		**TO DO**		MEETINGS	
				SEMINARS	
				CLASSES	
				PR'S SENT	
				FOLLOWUPS	

Week of_____

MONDAY	TUESDAY	WEDNESDAY
8am	8am	8am
10	10	10
12	12	12
2	2	2
4	4	4
6	6	6
8pm	8pm	8pm
TO DO	TO DO	TO DO

Thomas Edison's teachers said he was too stupid to learn anything.

THURSDAY		FRIDAY		SATURDAY	
8am		8am			
10		10			
12		12			
				SUNDAY	
2		2			
4		4			
6		6			
8pm		8pm		**WEEKLY TALLIES**	
				AUDITIONS	
				CALLBACKS	
TO DO		TO DO		MEETINGS	
				SEMINARS	
				CLASSES	
				PR'S SENT	
				FOLLOWUPS	

Week of_____

MONDAY		TUESDAY		WEDNESDAY	
8am		8am		8am	
10		10		10	
12		12		12	
2		2		2	
4		4		4	
6		6		6	
8pm		8pm		8pm	
TO DO		TO DO		TO DO	

M*A*S*H* was turned down by 21 publishers until finally the author, Richard Hooker, published it himself. It became a runaway bestseller, spawning a blockbuster movie and one of the most successful series' in television history.

THURSDAY	FRIDAY	SATURDAY
8am	8am	
10	10	
12	12	
		SUNDAY
2	2	
4	4	
6	6	
8pm	8pm	**WEEKLY TALLIES**
		AUDITIONS
		CALLBACKS
TO DO	TO DO	MEETINGS
		SEMINARS
		CLASSES
		PR'S SENT
		FOLLOWUPS

Week of_____

MONDAY		TUESDAY		WEDNESDAY	
8am		8am		8am	
10		10		10	
12		12		12	
2		2		2	
4		4		4	
6		6		6	
8pm		8pm		8pm	
TO DO		TO DO		TO DO	

The original version of The Organized Actor® was created in just three days.

THURSDAY		FRIDAY		SATURDAY	
8am		8am			
10		10			
12		12			
				SUNDAY	
2		2			
4		4			
6		6			
8pm		8pm		**WEEKLY TALLIES**	
TO DO		**TO DO**		AUDITIONS	
				CALLBACKS	
				MEETINGS	
				SEMINARS	
				CLASSES	
				PR'S SENT	
				FOLLOWUPS	

Week of_____

MONDAY		TUESDAY		WEDNESDAY	
8am		8am		8am	
10		10		10	
12		12		12	
2		2		2	
4		4		4	
6		6		6	
8pm		8pm		8pm	
TO DO		TO DO		TO DO	

Albert Einstein didn't speak until he was 4 years old and didn't read until he was 7. His teacher described him as "mentally slow, unsociable and forever adrift in his foolish dreams." He was expelled from Zurich Polytechnic School.

THURSDAY		FRIDAY		SATURDAY	
8am		8am			
10		10			
12		12			
				SUNDAY	
2		2			
4		4			
6		6			
8pm		8pm		**WEEKLY TALLIES**	
				AUDITIONS	
				CALLBACKS	
TO DO		**TO DO**		MEETINGS	
				SEMINARS	
				CLASSES	
				PR'S SENT	
				FOLLOWUPS	

Week of_____

MONDAY		TUESDAY		WEDNESDAY	
8am		8am		8am	
10		10		10	
12		12		12	
2		2		2	
4		4		4	
6		6		6	
8pm		8pm		8pm	
TO DO		TO DO		TO DO	

Anything is possible if only you believe.

THURSDAY		FRIDAY		SATURDAY	
8am		8am			
10		10			
12		12			
				SUNDAY	
2		2			
4		4			
6		6			
8pm		8pm		**WEEKLY TALLIES**	
				AUDITIONS	
				CALLBACKS	
TO DO		TO DO		MEETINGS	
				SEMINARS	
				CLASSES	
				PR'S SENT	
				FOLLOWUPS	

Week of_____

MONDAY		TUESDAY		WEDNESDAY	
8am		8am		8am	
10		10		10	
12		12		12	
2		2		2	
4		4		4	
6		6		6	
8pm		8pm		8pm	
TO DO		TO DO		TO DO	

Anything is possible if only you believe....and take some action.

THURSDAY		FRIDAY		SATURDAY	
8am		8am			
10		10			
12		12			
				SUNDAY	
2		2			
4		4			
6		6			
8pm		8pm		**WEEKLY TALLIES**	
				AUDITIONS	
				CALLBACKS	
TO DO		TO DO		MEETINGS	
				SEMINARS	
				CLASSES	
				PR'S SENT	
				FOLLOWUPS	

Week of_____

MONDAY	TUESDAY	WEDNESDAY
8am	8am	8am
10	10	10
12	12	12
2	2	2
4	4	4
6	6	6
8pm	8pm	8pm
TO DO	**TO DO**	**TO DO**

Be brave enough to declare, "This is who I am.
This is what I want.
And this is how I'm going to get it!"

THURSDAY	FRIDAY	SATURDAY
8am	8am	
10	10	
12	12	
		SUNDAY
2	2	
4	4	
6	6	
8pm	8pm	**WEEKLY TALLIES**
		AUDITIONS
		CALLBACKS
TO DO	**TO DO**	MEETINGS
		SEMINARS
		CLASSES
		PR'S SENT
		FOLLOWUPS

Week of_____

MONDAY		TUESDAY		WEDNESDAY	
8am		8am		8am	
10		10		10	
12		12		12	
2		2		2	
4		4		4	
6		6		6	
8pm		8pm		8pm	
TO DO		TO DO		TO DO	

Never give up on your dreams.

THURSDAY		FRIDAY		SATURDAY	
8am		8am			
10		10			
12		12			
2		2		**SUNDAY**	
4		4			
6		6			
8pm		8pm		**WEEKLY TALLIES**	

TO DO   **TO DO**

AUDITIONS

CALLBACKS

MEETINGS

SEMINARS

CLASSES

PR'S SENT

FOLLOWUPS

Week of_____

MONDAY	TUESDAY	WEDNESDAY
8am	8am	8am
10	10	10
12	12	12
2	2	2
4	4	4
6	6	6
8pm	8pm	8pm
TO DO	TO DO	TO DO

Watch out for sour blueberries.

THURSDAY		FRIDAY		SATURDAY	
8am		8am			
10		10			
12		12			
				SUNDAY	
2		2			
4		4			
6		6			
8pm		8pm		**WEEKLY TALLIES**	
				AUDITIONS	
				CALLBACKS	
TO DO		**TO DO**		MEETINGS	
				SEMINARS	
				CLASSES	
				PR'S SENT	
				FOLLOWUPS	

Week of_____

MONDAY	TUESDAY	WEDNESDAY
8am	8am	8am
10	10	10
12	12	12
2	2	2
4	4	4
6	6	6
8pm	8pm	8pm
TO DO	TO DO	TO DO

There is no more perfect moment than now.

THURSDAY		FRIDAY		SATURDAY	
8am		8am			
10		10			
12		12		**SUNDAY**	
2		2			
4		4			
6		6			
8pm		8pm		**WEEKLY TALLIES**	
				AUDITIONS	
				CALLBACKS	
TO DO		TO DO		MEETINGS	
				SEMINARS	
				CLASSES	
				PR'S SENT	
				FOLLOWUPS	

Week of_____

MONDAY	TUESDAY	WEDNESDAY
8am	8am	8am
10	10	10
12	12	12
2	2	2
4	4	4
6	6	6
8pm	8pm	8pm
TO DO	TO DO	TO DO

"Circumstance does not make the man. It reveals him to himself."

James Allen, As a Man Thinketh

THURSDAY		FRIDAY		SATURDAY	
8am		8am			
10		10			
12		12			
2		2		**SUNDAY**	
4		4			
6		6			
8pm		8pm		**WEEKLY TALLIES**	
				AUDITIONS	
				CALLBACKS	
TO DO		TO DO		MEETINGS	
				SEMINARS	
				CLASSES	
				PR'S SENT	
				FOLLOWUPS	

Week of_____

MONDAY	TUESDAY	WEDNESDAY
8am	8am	8am
10	10	10
12	12	12
2	2	2
4	4	4
6	6	6
8pm	8pm	8pm
TO DO	TO DO	TO DO

There's always someone to admire, and someone who admires you.

THURSDAY	FRIDAY	SATURDAY
8am	8am	
10	10	
12	12	
		SUNDAY
2	2	
4	4	
6	6	
8pm	8pm	**WEEKLY TALLIES**
		AUDITIONS
		CALLBACKS
TO DO	TO DO	MEETINGS
		SEMINARS
		CLASSES
		PR'S SENT
		FOLLOWUPS

Week of_____

MONDAY	TUESDAY	WEDNESDAY
8am	8am	8am
10	10	10
12	12	12
2	2	2
4	4	4
6	6	6
8pm	8pm	8pm
TO DO	TO DO	TO DO

Be your word.

THURSDAY	FRIDAY	SATURDAY
8am	8am	
10	10	
12	12	
2	2	**SUNDAY**
4	4	
6	6	
8pm	8pm	**WEEKLY TALLIES**

WEEKLY TALLIES

AUDITIONS

CALLBACKS

MEETINGS

SEMINARS

CLASSES

PR'S SENT

FOLLOWUPS

TO DO

TO DO

Week of_____

MONDAY	TUESDAY	WEDNESDAY
8am	8am	8am
10	10	10
12	12	12
2	2	2
4	4	4
6	6	6
8pm	8pm	8pm
TO DO	TO DO	TO DO

Don't take anything personally.

THURSDAY		FRIDAY		SATURDAY	
8am		8am			
10		10			
12		12			
				SUNDAY	
2		2			
4		4			
6		6			
8pm		8pm		**WEEKLY TALLIES**	
				AUDITIONS	
				CALLBACKS	
TO DO		**TO DO**		MEETINGS	
				SEMINARS	
				CLASSES	
				PR'S SENT	
				FOLLOWUPS	

Week of_____

MONDAY	TUESDAY	WEDNESDAY
8am	8am	8am
10	10	10
12	12	12
2	2	2
4	4	4
6	6	6
8pm	8pm	8pm
TO DO	TO DO	TO DO

Be a human being, then an actor.

THURSDAY		FRIDAY		SATURDAY	
8am		8am			
10		10			
12		12			
				SUNDAY	
2		2			
4		4			
6		6			
8pm		8pm		**WEEKLY TALLIES**	
				AUDITIONS	
				CALLBACKS	
TO DO		**TO DO**		MEETINGS	
				SEMINARS	
				CLASSES	
				PR'S SENT	
				FOLLOWUPS	

Week of_____

MONDAY	TUESDAY	WEDNESDAY
8am	8am	8am
10	10	10
12	12	12
2	2	2
4	4	4
6	6	6
8pm	8pm	8pm
TO DO	TO DO	TO DO

Love thyself.

THURSDAY	FRIDAY	SATURDAY
8am	8am	
10	10	
12	12	
		SUNDAY
2	2	
4	4	
6	6	
8pm	8pm	**WEEKLY TALLIES**

WEEKLY TALLIES

AUDITIONS ☐

CALLBACKS ☐

MEETINGS ☐

SEMINARS ☐

CLASSES ☐

PR'S SENT ☐

FOLLOWUPS ☐

TO DO

TO DO

Week of_____

MONDAY	TUESDAY	WEDNESDAY
8am	8am	8am
10	10	10
12	12	12
2	2	2
4	4	4
6	6	6
8pm	8pm	8pm
TO DO	TO DO	TO DO

Whether you think you can or think you can't, you're right.

THURSDAY		FRIDAY		SATURDAY	
8am		8am			
10		10			
12		12			
				SUNDAY	
2		2			
4		4			
6		6			
8pm		8pm		**WEEKLY TALLIES**	
				AUDITIONS	
				CALLBACKS	
TO DO		TO DO		MEETINGS	
				SEMINARS	
				CLASSES	
				PR'S SENT	
				FOLLOWUPS	

Week of_____

MONDAY	TUESDAY	WEDNESDAY
8am	8am	8am
10	10	10
12	12	12
2	2	2
4	4	4
6	6	6
8pm	8pm	8pm
TO DO	TO DO	TO DO

Your being small never serves anyone.

THURSDAY		FRIDAY		SATURDAY	

THURSDAY

8am

10

12

2

4

6

8pm

TO DO

FRIDAY

8am

10

12

2

4

6

8pm

TO DO

SATURDAY

SUNDAY

WEEKLY TALLIES

AUDITIONS ☐

CALLBACKS ☐

MEETINGS ☐

SEMINARS ☐

CLASSES ☐

PR'S SENT ☐

FOLLOWUPS ☐

Week of_____

MONADAY	TUESDAY	WEDNESDAY
8am	8am	8am
10	10	10
12	12	12
2	2	2
4	4	4
6	6	6
8pm	8pm	8pm
TO DO	**TO DO**	**TO DO**

The secret to success? Showing up.

THURSDAY	FRIDAY	SATURDAY
8am	8am	
10	10	
12	12	
		SUNDAY
2	2	
4	4	
6	6	
8pm	8pm	**WEEKLY TALLIES**

WEEKLY TALLIES

AUDITIONS ☐

CALLBACKS ☐

MEETINGS ☐

SEMINARS ☐

CLASSES ☐

PR'S SENT ☐

FOLLOWUPS ☐

TO DO

TO DO

Week of_____

MONDAY		TUESDAY		WEDNESDAY	
8am		8am		8am	
10		10		10	
12		12		12	
2		2		2	
4		4		4	
6		6		6	
8pm		8pm		8pm	
TO DO		TO DO		TO DO	

They can't know what you can do unless you show them.

THURSDAY		FRIDAY		SATURDAY	
8am		8am			
10		10			
12		12			
2		2		**SUNDAY**	
4		4			
6		6			
8pm		8pm		**WEEKLY TALLIES**	

TO DO

TO DO

WEEKLY TALLIES

AUDITIONS ☐

CALLBACKS ☐

MEETINGS ☐

SEMINARS ☐

CLASSES ☐

PR'S SENT ☐

FOLLOWUPS ☐

Week of_____

MONDAY	TUESDAY	WEDNESDAY
8am	8am	8am
10	10	10
12	12	12
2	2	2
4	4	4
6	6	6
8pm	8pm	8pm
TO DO	TO DO	TO DO

Live! Laugh! Love!

THURSDAY	FRIDAY	SATURDAY
8am	8am	
10	10	
12	12	
		SUNDAY
2	2	
4	4	
6	6	
8pm	8pm	**WEEKLY TALLIES**
		AUDITIONS
		CALLBACKS
TO DO	TO DO	MEETINGS
		SEMINARS
		CLASSES
		PR'S SENT
		FOLLOWUPS

Week of_____

MONDAY		TUESDAY		WEDNESDAY	
8am		8am		8am	
10		10		10	
12		12		12	
2		2		2	
4		4		4	
6		6		6	
8pm		8pm		8pm	
TO DO		TO DO		TO DO	

Be braver than you think you are.

THURSDAY		FRIDAY		SATURDAY	
8am		8am			
10		10			
12		12			
2		2		**SUNDAY**	
4		4			
6		6			
8pm		8pm		**WEEKLY TALLIES**	
TO DO		**TO DO**		AUDITIONS	
				CALLBACKS	
				MEETINGS	
				SEMINARS	
				CLASSES	
				PR'S SENT	
				FOLLOWUPS	

Week of _____

MONDAY	TUESDAY	WEDNESDAY
8am	8am	8am
10	10	10
12	12	12
2	2	2
4	4	4
6	6	6
8pm	8pm	8pm
TO DO	TO DO	TO DO

"Imagine all the people living life in peace" John Lennon

THURSDAY		FRIDAY		SATURDAY	
8am		8am			
10		10			
12		12			
				SUNDAY	
2		2			
4		4			
6		6			
8pm		8pm		**WEEKLY TALLIES**	
TO DO		**TO DO**		AUDITIONS	
				CALLBACKS	
				MEETINGS	
				SEMINARS	
				CLASSES	
				PR'S SENT	
				FOLLOWUPS	

A Year of Planning

JANUARY	FEBRUARY	MARCH
APRIL	MAY	JUNE
JULY	AUGUST	SEPTEMBER
OCTOBER	NOVEMBER	DECEMBER

A Year in Review

At the end of each year, it's important to reflect back on what the year has been about, what you learned and what you achieved. When you're finished with this copy of The Organized Actor®, take a moment to reflect on how far you've come this year!

1. What accomplishment are you most proud of this year?

2. What specific goal made you the happiest to achieve?

3. What did you learn this year?

4. What goal has still eluded you?

5. Did you make any new lifelong friends this year?

6. What did you learn to love about yourself this year?

7. What fear did you overcome this year?

8. What was your favorite acting moment this year?

Tally Totals

This year I went on   _____   auditions

I was calledback   _____   times

I had meetings with   _____   industry pros

I took   _____   seminars

I took   _____   classes

I sent out   _____   headshots

About our Company....

Triple Threat Ventures, LLC was founded by Leslie Becker in 1988. The purpose of the company is to inspire, educate and entertain others, and to add value to their lives as performers and people. We are dedicated to helping others continue their quest for stardom in all areas of their lives.

We specialize in motivational and organizational products for Actors and Artists including

Books
Audio Programs
E-courses
Career Coaching
Motivational Newsletters
Mailing Service
and more...

Our Automated Mailing Service
Tired of licking, stamping and addressing your postcard mailings to agents and casting directors? Look not further! Check out our mailing service that allows you to SEND REAL CARDS IN THE REAL MAIL at the touch of a button. You can load up your headshots and send cards anytime you need to!
Check it out at www.OrganizedActor.com

Work IT! Newsletter
Tips for Workin' Your Acting Career and Your Life
Sign up for FREE at www.OrganizedActor.com

New! Fool Proof Goal Setting Audio Program
Now you can "attend" Leslie's live seminar from the comforts of your own home with this powerful new Audio Program. Get her complete Fool Proof Goal Setting Seminar in an action-packed, interactive program that includes her "life-altering" visualization, complete goal setting workshop and your own Fool Proof Guidebook! Order today at www.OrganizedActor.com

www.OrganizedActor.com
We're organized, so you don't have to be!